Arise & SHINE

Visionary Author - Dr. Tonia M. Blackwood
Foreword - Dr. Nichole Peters

KINGDOM
PUBLISHING

We would like to acknowledge the authors of the following materials for permission to print their work:

Arise & Shine: It's a Requirement, Not an Option! Reprinted by permission of Dr. Tonia M. Blackwood © 2022 Dr. Tonia M. Blackwood

A Leap of Faith Reprinted by permission of Baneshia Wyatt © 2022 Baneshia Wyatt

Who Is Carrying the Black Bag? Reprinted by permission of Leolene Hines © 2022 Leolene Hines

Quick and in a Hurry Reprinted by permission of Dr. Dorissa McCalister © 2022 Dr. Dorissa McCalister

Goin' Up Yonder Reprinted by permission of Dr. Felice Kelly Gillum © 2022 Dr. Felice Kelly Gillum

Arise and Walk by Faith in Real Time! Reprinted by permission of Jean Turner © 2022 Jean Turner

Rising from Brokenness Reprinted by permission of Von M. Giggs © 2022 Von M. Griggs

Be Relentless Reprinted by permission of Nicole D. Roberts © 2022 Nicole D. Roberts

Overcomers Reborn By Faith Reprinted by permission of Dr. Judy Ambrose James © 2022 Dr. Judy Ambrose James

The Struggle Within Me Reprinted by permission of Sentretta Brumfield-Baity © 2022 Sentretta Brumfield-Baity

Prepared for a Comeback Reprinted by permission of Theresa F. Thompson © 2022 Theresa Thompson

One Decision Can Change Everything Reprinted by permission of Shawn Casey Collins Jr. © 2022 Shawn Casey Collins Jr.

ISBN 978-1-7375156-4-7 (print) | ISBN 978-1-7375156-5-4 (ebook)

Cover Design: Rob Williams

Scriptures and additional materials marked (GNT) are from the Good News Bible © 1994 published by the Bible Societies/HarperCollins Publishers Ltd UK, Good News Bible© American Bible Society 1966, 1971, 1976, 1992. Used with permission.

Some scriptures taken from the King James Version (KJV) are part of the public domain.

Scripture quotations marked (NIV) are taken from the Holy Bible, New International Version®, NIV®. Copyright © 1973, 1978, 1984, 2011 by Biblica, Inc.™ Used by permission of Zondervan. All rights reserved worldwide. www.zondervan.comThe "NIV" and "New International Version" are trademarks registered in the United States Patent and Trademark Office by Biblica, Inc.™

Scripture marked (NKJV) taken from the New King James Version®. Copyright © 1982 by Thomas Nelson. Used by permission. All rights reserved.

Scripture quotations marked (NLT) are taken from the Holy Bible, New Living Translation, copyright ©1996, 2004, 2015 by Tyndale House Foundation. Used by permission of Tyndale House Publishers, Carol Stream, Illinois 60188. All rights reserved.

Dedication

To Markelda Rankin and Sidney A. Blackwood Sr.—
You both enable me to make the decision to **RISE** every day! Even when everything around me says not to, I continue to seek God's face because of what you deposited in me. Your undeniable tenacity and pure determination are a gift you wrapped in a bow for all your children, and I am forever grateful to you both. Although you came to America separately, your union has created a shining light for so many. I love you with my whole heart.

To each author in this collection—
Thank you for your yes and your courage!

To all those who opened my eyes to what life can offer if we just *GET UP*—
Thank you for praying and encouraging me on this journey to *RISE*!

And most importantly, thank you to my Creator who continues to heal, bless, cover, and consistently love me in spite of my missteps. He is my ultimate reason to *ARISE & SHINE!*

Table of Contents

Foreword

By Dr. Nichole E. Peters

Hear ye, hear ye!

It's time for you to read all about why it is time for *you* to *rise up* so you can shine. There is a sense of emergency in your life at this very moment. So many people feel like they are at their very lowest. Many are barely breathing, unsure that with everything happening in this world we will ever recover and get back up. In the past couple of years, we all have been aware of many people losing their lives, including some of our own loved ones, neighbors, and friends. Many people to this day are still fighting for their lives to go back to some sense of normalcy after losing their careers and jobs due to COVID-19. The suicide rate has doubled even in our younger generation, marriages across America are failing, and divorces have tripled; in addition, mental illness is at an all-time high and soaring like never before. That's why this anthology is here: to help you snatch your power back by knowing with God you can *arise* by using the light that is deep inside you. Father God tells us in the good book that no one can snatch us out of His almighty powerful hands. It's time to *shine* like never before, and this is what every chapter in this book will convince you to do.

Father God tells us in Matthew 5:16 (KJV), "Let your light so shine before men, that they may see your good works, and glorify your Father which is in heaven." My brothers and sisters, do you know what a powerful position you're in? Choose to *arise* on this day and *shine*! You're covered under the wings of the Almighty and Most High. When we just stand still, take authority, and let God fight for us (Exodus 14:14), there is no darkness and no hell that can keep you down, hostage, or dead. Let the healing words from each amazing author in this book help you to overcome all obstacles, darkness, and distress. Will it be easy? NO! Nothing comes easy when there's greatness attached to it. Will it be worth it? Oh yes! Stay in the grit by trusting God and the leaders whom He has appointed in your life to help bring you many blessings. Stay obedient to the living Word of God and in good company. If the authors in this book can *arise* through it all, so can you!

Even the amazing visionary of this anthology, Dr. Tonia M. Blackwood, thought it was over for her after being diagnosed with two brain aneurysms, and she didn't know if she was going to live or die...but God! Take me, for another example; I can attest to the same thing. I was extremely sick and went through three different surgeries in one year. I was also on fourteen different medications including two that had to be delivered and signed for from a specialty pharmacy because of the composition of the medication. I felt like I was dying and would be dead soon. I had even started planning my own funeral! However, what I had to realize is that the power of God can even heal the dead. Jehovah Rappa was my healer, like He was for many others you will soon read about.

You see, the God we serve can bring anyone back from anything they're going through—even from the dead. In the New Testament, Jesus Christ healed many who were dead. Let me name a few. In the book of Luke, onlookers laughed at Jesus for saying that the young girl was sleeping and not dead. Jesus even told Jairus, "Don't be afraid; just believe" (Luke 8:50 NIV). And soon the mourning of Jairus's daughter was turned into praise and worship!

In another example from the book of Acts is Tabitha. She was like so many others who were loved and respected in their cities (Acts 9:36–42). In the great city of Joppa, Tabitha, whose name is Dorcas in Greek, rocked with her city. What does that mean? She was always doing good, always helping others, especially the poor, and making garments for her people. Tabitha ended up growing sick and dying, and the whole city mourned the death of this amazing woman of God. After the women washed her body, laid her out in preparation for burial, they sent for the apostle Peter who wasn't that far from them. Peter made it there, cleared out the room, and got on his knees and prayed out to the Lord Jesus Christ to heal her. Peter then told Tabitha to get up, and Tabitha sat up! As a result, many of their friends and so many others started believing in Jesus.

Last but not least, when Lazarus, one of Jesus's closest friends, died, even Jesus wept about his friend dying; He showed His emotions even though He knew He would bring Lazarus back to life. Lazarus had been dead for four days before the Son of God made His way to him. Jesus took His time getting there, maybe to calm the tensions of the many who wanted Him killed; aware that Jesus was noted to be close to the city where Lazarus's tomb was located. When Jesus got there, He commanded that the tombstone be removed, and everyone witnessed Lazarus *arise*.

We all must realize that God is the resurrector of life. It's doesn't matter what we've been through, what our lives look like, or even if we've reached rock bottom.

With God, if you choose to *arise*, you can go from rock bottom to rocking the world! Are you ready to *rise*? Are you ready to *shine*? Are you ready to *believe* that you've got what it takes to do both?

Greater is He who is inside you, and the power to be the greatest is inside us all! Each story in this anthology will bring more light into your life as you witness the evidence of God's miracles performed.

Now is your time! Now is your moment! Learn from each writer how the Lord Jesus Christ can turn it all around for you. Let me ask you a question: Are you going to believe God and the miracles in this book? Or will you listen to your doubts that feed your fear? Remember, no matter what your life looks like, you can *arise and shine* through it all—from depression, darkness, grief, sickness, hopelessness, divorce, miscarriage, abuse, insanity, and more. How? By knowing that even if you feel like it's over for you and the pressure from the dead weight is building momentum and wearing you down, Father God can bring you out of anything because He is our *arisen* King!

Arise...Arise...Arise. Now is your time to bloom where you are planted and shine like never before. May God bless us all!

CONNECT WITH DR. DR. NICHOLE E. PETERS

f @nicolewomenoflpr

@ @believeinyourdreamstv

Arise & Shine: It's a Requirement, Not an Option!

By Dr. Tonia M. Blackwood

"You don't drown by falling in the water; you drown by staying there."
—Edwin Louis Cole

Do you ever think, *No! I don't want to get up! I'm tired!* So very tired and not feeling like you want to move from whatever position you're in. For me, it was just the simple act of standing up. You see I was recovering from brain surgery and the slightest change in levels would really make my head hurt. However, if I'm being transparent, it was my heart that was hurting me even more. I was reeling from the fact that I wasn't even fifty years old yet and recovering from my second brain surgery. Besides the physical pain, I was feeling defeated and weak in mind, body, and spirit.

If you close your eyes, you can see your own version of the "woe is me" film I was watching. The many mistakes and errors in judgment that had brought me to this place. Putting my health on the back burner, or real talk, making my company my God. I was really getting into the movie too...I mean, popcorn with extra butter into my movie! Can we be honest with ourselves and say that sometimes we experience difficulties and may spend a moment or two watching our life movie play out? But God! Do some of us even get stuck there, only realizing years later the precious time we wasted? Could it be that those movies become the very foundation that our limiting beliefs are built on?

Perhaps we are asking ourselves the wrong questions:

- Who is going to sign up for this life with me?
- What if they find out I'm not perfect?
- What if I'm not strong enough to deal with the rejection that comes from putting myself out there?

As I write this, my spirit is stirring because the woman God has brought from that dark place of pity is so different today. Up to that point, I hadn't stopped to think hard about where God had brought me from—including surviving the dangerous surgery I was recovering from. My thoughts should have been about the *victory* instead of about darkness and defeat. My attitude should have been one of undeniable *gratitude* even in my pain. I should have been in a posture of continuous praise. How often do you hear about someone just dropping dead from one brain aneurysm? However, this child of God had *not one* but *two* aneurysms diagonally across from each other and through God's grace survived them both by having a gifted believer (my surgeon) seal them. I was blessed to *rise* again to see the *light* of another day.

So why would I choose to focus on what I perceived as broken? The answer is simple: I lost my way, I tripped and fell, and it was the very voice of God that *woke* me and enabled me to see *His* extended hand. In my spirit I heard, *"How dare you?" Don't you remember whose you are? Get up and fight! You are made from me. You are a masterpiece and I'm not done yet!"* Tough love, right? But always with the hand extended to help me if I chose to accept it and grab on.

Even though I knew God and was (against doctor's orders) stubborn enough to attend a women's spiritual empowerment conference shortly after my procedure, I let my limiting beliefs slip in and take over once again. Yes, you can know Him and still have doubts. It is true that in the quiet moments you can drown out the voice of God with noise and distractions. However, the key to overcoming your limiting beliefs and the ones that others project on you is to stay connected and armed with the weapons of warfare: the Word and continuous prayer. These should serve as your sword and shield. The Bible speaks directly to the power that comes from putting on the full armor of God:

Finally, be strong in the Lord and in his mighty power. Put on the full armor of God, so that you can take your stand against the devil's schemes. For our struggle is not against flesh and blood, but against the rulers, against the authorities, against the powers of this dark world and against the spiritual forces of evil in the heavenly realms. Therefore put on the full armor of God, so that when the day of evil comes, you may be able to stand your ground, and after you have done everything, to stand. Stand firm then, with the belt of truth buckled around your waist, with the breastplate of righteousness in place, and with your feet fitted with the readiness that comes from the gospel of peace. In addition to all this, take up the shield of faith, with which you can extinguish all the flaming arrows of the evil one. Take the helmet of salvation and the sword of the Spirit, which is the word of God. And pray in the Spirit on all occasions with all kinds of prayers and requests. With this in mind, be alert and always keep on praying for all the Lord's people. (Ephesians 6:10–18 NIV)

During that time in my life, I was feeling so weak that I forgot His strength was the reason I was still breathing. I forgot that if I prayed continuously in faith, my shield would block any "stinking thinking" that my flesh could get exposed to! I've learned two very important things over the years:

1. Stay armed and ready! Stay in the Word!

- What does the Bible say about who you are?
  - o You are a conqueror; you are the head, not the tail, a lender and not a borrower!

- What does the Bible say about your capabilities?
  - o You can do all things through Christ Jesus! (Philippians 4:13).

- Finally, what does the Bible really say about your responsibility?
  - o There are so many examples in the Bible that show us what can happen when we do the work and not try to avoid the process. The

Word is full of verbs, and it's no coincidence that many, if not all, of the miracles performed by Jesus started with an action (verb) he commanded first.

- "Then Jesus said to him, 'Get up! Pick up your mat and walk'" (John 5:8 NIV).
- "Now get up and go into the city, and you will be told what you must do" (Acts 9:6 NIV).
- "Get yourself ready! Stand up and say to them whatever I command you. Do not be terrified by them, or I will terrify you before them" (Jeremiah 1:17 NIV).

  Sometimes scary, He must give us a nudge, like any good parent. I had to learn that the promises of God always require an investment. There is no bargaining or negotiating your contribution to the process. Just like any great prize you must participate to win!

2. Ask yourself the right questions to annihilate the limiting beliefs!

- What is really me holding me back from having the life I desire?
- What beliefs create these obstacles for me?
- Where do they come from? What's the root of my negative thoughts?
- Do I really think these beliefs are true?
- How do I overcome these challenges?

Now, there will be times when *you* are not the one to ask these questions. Or you may not be in a good place to get the answers you need or handle the answers you do come up with. That's when a good coach or therapist is necessary for you to level up so you can *arise and shine*! We are not meant to do this life alone. Staying armed and ready is the first step because it's foundational. It is your spiritual DNA. Being rooted and grounded will enable you to answer whatever questions this world throws you or give you the discernment to seek the help you need.

Remember, Isaiah 60:1 (NIV) says, "Arise, shine, for your light has come, and the glory of the LORD rises upon you." There are no other options offered. You must arise and shine in order to be the light so that others can see that the glory of the Lord rises upon you. He is counting on you and me to be an example and to build the kingdom. It is a requirement!

CONNECT WITH DR. TONIA M. BLACKWOOD

f @toniablackwood & @thenirise

📷 @toniablackwood & @thenirise

in @tmblackwood

🌐 www.toniablackwood.com

A Leap of Faith
By Baneshia Wyatt

"Change will not come if we wait for some other person or some other time. We are the ones we've been waiting for. We are the change that we seek."
—Barak Obama

As I packed the car, a tsunami of doubt came rushing in, and I began interrogating myself.

Baneshia, are you sure? What are you doing? You're leaving everything you know. Are you sure you heard God's voice?

I can't believe it's four months into 2013, and it's already proven to be one of the most monumental years of my life. It's all happening so quick. I think I am in shock. Six months ago, I returned from a mini vacation with my children to Charlotte, North Carolina. Some friends had invited us down. They knew I was going through an awful separation from my ex-husband, and I needed a reprieve from the hustle and bustle of life. I was mentally overwhelmed and emotionally exhausted. I needed a break.

As the kids and I arrived on the Greyhound bus and peered out the window, my spirit was leaping like the baby in Elizabeth's belly when Elizabeth met Jesus's mother Mary. There was something magical about this place; I felt like Alice in Wonderland. The scenery was breathtaking, the air was crisp, and the people were charming. It was one of the best decisions I could have ever made. We ate well, worshipped freely, the kids swam and enjoyed so many activities they couldn't do back home. It was so relaxing, I felt like I was in a whole new world. By the time we were to head home, I had gained a second wind, but I also knew I had to go back and face some hard truths and make some tough decisions. I went back home, and I could not get Charlotte out of my mind for weeks. I felt a pull I couldn't explain, and Rochester no longer felt like home or where I belonged. I had to make sure I was thinking rationally. I knew I was in a vulnerable state, and I understood the importance of not making major decisions while my emotions were on a roller coaster.

After many months of praying and fasting, waiting to hear from God, He spoke. *"I am sending you out like Abram."* The Lord had instructed me to quit my job and move to Charlotte, North Carolina, where the only people I knew were the couple I had previously visited. I thought, *God, what does Abram have to do with me?* As soon as I asked the question, God led me to Genesis 12:1–3. In the NLT it reads, "The LORD had said to Abram, 'L eave your native country, your relatives, and your father's family, and go to the land that I will show you. I will make you into a great nation." I knew it was Him because it penetrated my soul.

These instructions didn't make sense. I still had questions about whether my marriage would be reconciled or if it was going to end in divorce. I had lived in the same city for over thirty years, had no job prospects and only limited funds in my bank account. I found myself as a single mom with two children. The only guarantee I had was the promise the Lord gave me.

For the first time in my life, I didn't have the plan all mapped out. I had moved out of my mom's home at seventeen, so I was no stranger to making things happen. However, this time I wasn't in control, which was extremely scary. I could no longer rely on my finite wisdom. I had to put my faith to the test. I had to trust in God.

This is what you call blind faith. I was in the deep, yet I had resounding confidence that I was doing the right thing. When I began to share what the Lord was instructing me to do, unsolicited comments came in many different forms. "Baneshia, you're running from your marital problems." Or "We're not worried, you'll be back soon." And I could never forget this one: "you're crazy, I could never do that."

These responses weren't making me feel any better, especially since I didn't fully understand it all myself. A few others were very encouraging, but I had made up in my mind that it didn't matter what people thought, including myself. I was just desperate for change and knew I had to be obedient. Breaking this news to my mother was a whole different story. Although I had left home at an early age, my mom and I were extremely close. As I drove to her house to tell her, there was great trepidation in my heart. I played the scenario over and over in my head. I had butterflies in my stomach, and I felt sick, but no matter what, my mom's approval would not be required for this next season. When I arrived, we greeted each other with our usual hug and sat on the couch. I shared what God had instructed me to do.

There was a long moment of silence. Next, to my surprise, Mom uttered, "Honey, if God told you to go, who am I to stop you?"

I was shocked. Her response was confirmation this was the Holy Spirit.

However, even with the divine confirmation from my mother's response, I still had questions. How are my kids going to adjust? What support system will I have? What if I don't find a job? I was terrified, but I kept moving forward. God, so concerned and caring, continued to use different people and events to confirm the plans He had for me. One evening my best friend invited me to a church service with a well-known prophet. Despite the fact he didn't know me, he picked me out of a large crowd and said God is leading you to move, and when you get there, a Caucasian woman that you will befriend is going to help you with a home, and you are going to get a new car. This prophetic word encouraged me. God was giving me a sneak peek that many blessings were tied to my obedience in this move.

I took a leap of faith even with my uncertainties, fears, and lack of a job. It was a divine setup from the Lord! My friends were kind enough to do all the legwork for me in Charlotte and secured an apartment for us, which I didn't even see until I arrived. My mom even graciously drove me to my new city and stayed with me to get settled in.

When I arrived, it wasn't anything like I expected. I thought it was going to be smooth sailing. Often when God gives you a promise, He leaves out the in-between. I wish I could tell you I stepped into Charlotte and the waters parted and everything was seamless. The truth is it was hard. My apartment wasn't ready, and I didn't land a permanent job for nine months. I felt incredibly lonely and like I had regressed. However, I still somehow knew this was the right decision and going back was not an option. The Lord kept reminding me that I was in a stripping process. He was building my faith and dependency on Him, but it all would be rewarded. As I continued to seek the Lord, He gave me specific instructions: dating was off-limits, and abstinence was required. I didn't understand it because I was still married. I wasn't thinking about a man or sex, but the Lord knew I needed to settle that in my heart so my attention wouldn't be divided. I wanted to be whole, and I knew it would take work on my part, but I was all in. I was done doing things my way. I was committed to living holy and surrendered to God.

Abstinence brought me clarity in who I was and what I needed to work on. I attended a divorce program at church. I learned about soul ties, father wounds, abandonment, and rejection issues.

I made my healing a priority. Both my children and I attended therapy. I took numerous seminars, read books, and went through deliverance. God created the most amazing support system to help me and hold me accountable. My obedience to God landed me a great job, which I still hold sixteen years later. The prophet's word came to pass. I did meet a Caucasian woman who blessed me with a brand-new car, fully paid for, and who helped me purchase a home. I did *arise and shine*. I became a certified life/divorce recovery coach, minister, podcaster, author, and started a business, Prevailing Women Life Coaching LLC, where I coach women in their identity in Christ and in divorce recovery.

As I reflect on my journey, faith and dependence on God is the common theme. What is God asking you to do? Are you willing to take a leap of faith so you can *arise and shine* too?

CONNECT WITH BANESHIA WYATT

f @baneshia.wyatt.5

🌐 www.prevailingwomenlifecoaching.com

Arise & **SHINE**

Who Is Carrying the Black Bag?

By Leolene Hinds

"I have the strength to face all conditions by the power that Chris gives me."
—Philippians 4:13 (GNT)

There was a welcome silence as we embarked on our way home from church. Our daughter Ashley is a talker! Usually on the drive, she would become our teacher and share all she learned and experienced in her Sunday school class. However, on this warm summer day, this was not the case. Our daughter was painstakingly quiet, which I admit was a bit puzzling yet wonderful.

Five minutes after we left the church, the quietness was interrupted by a solemn yet loud bellow from Ashley. Her monologue began:

"I wish this was a movie that would come to an end."

"I wish this was a tick and I could just flick it off."

"I wish I could stay in the pool for hours with my dad."

"I wish this was a dream and when I awoke it would be over."

"I wish Mommy and I could go out for ice cream like normal."

"I wish I could eat desserts with by brothers."

"I want be normal like the other kids."

"I wish I could stop carrying this black bag."

She was halfway through the monologue when we caught on to what she was referencing. The dam had finally broken. The frustration and anger that had been building in her over the diagnosis she obtained in the latter half of fourth grade finally came out.

As I drove, I quietly rehearsed, reflected, and agreed with all her statements. In my mind, I added a statement of my own: I wish this was an infection that would clear up in a few days with medication.

It all began fourteen months prior when I had observed my daughter going to the bathroom excessively. She also was consuming an enormous amount of water and was constantly hungry. My concern heightened when she took three trips to the bathroom in the middle of the night. On the last trip my daughter wet herself. I was shocked! This eight-year-old child had not wet herself since she came out of diapers at eighteen months.

The entire ordeal was puzzling as I continued to observe this change in behavior. I recall early one Sunday morning expressing to my husband, "I think our daughter has type 1 diabetes." Once the words left my mouth, I was shocked at what I'd just said. I had no idea what type 1 diabetes was and didn't know anyone associated with the disease. In the Christian world we call this a "word of knowledge," which is the Holy Spirit giving insight to something you are not aware of.

I continued my day as normal, which included going to church. Even though my body was in the service, my mind was fixed on the conversation I'd had with my husband.

After church I decided to drive my daughter straight to urgent care, where I received the devastating news. The doctor came in and hesitantly echoed my words, "I suspect your daughter has type 1 diabetes. She needs to be transferred to our main hospital immediately."

My knees buckled beneath the weight of his words. The nurse rushed in to hold me up. Ironically, she knew my pain because her son was diagnosed with the same illness when he was six months old.

The doctor then shared these encouraging words. "You saved her life by bringing her in this afternoon. Her blood sugar is over six hundred." That is six times higher than the normal blood sugar range.

We spent the next five days in the hospital as my daughter underwent many tests before the chief endocrinologist confirmed our worst fear. My daughter was officially diagnosed as a type 1 diabetic.

While in the hospital, a friendly stranger came to visit. She reminded me of myself when I would call on people, I didn't know in the hospital to keep them company. Once she started questioning my family structure, it became odd. I later learned she was a social worker. I vividly recall her saying, "Don't neglect her, as this is a lifelong illness. At times, parents can get tired. If you get tired of taking care of her, call us and we will pick her up."

Righteous indignation coupled with anger rose up inside me. I responded poignantly, "This is my daughter, and you will never have to pick her up because of neglect." At that point, I asked her to kindly leave the room, as our conversation was now over.

This diagnosis changed everything! Our spontaneous trips to the ice cream parlor were replaced with sugar-free Jell-O at home. Pizza night with her brothers was replaced with carefully crafted home-cooked meals.

My goodness, I was not prepared for the number of needles involved in this process. And having to prick my own daughter...terrible. I was the mom who had my husband take our children to their doctor's appointment when shots were involved.

I had to be trained on how to prick her finger and administer insulin with needles many times a day. This was a required regimen before and after every meal. The black bag that housed her tester, insulin strips, and needles became more important than my red purse.

After further contemplation, I came to realize this was more than a medical issue for my daughter, but a shattering of my childhood dreams. In my family, there were many children who lived without their moms for various reasons. I remember being a little girl and admiring every mom-and-daughter relationship. I loved the togetherness and the camaraderie. It truly warmed my heart. I made a decision as a child that if I had a daughter, I would mirror these relationships.

As you can imagine, when my daughter was born, I began executing my childhood dream. She became my bosom buddy from day one. All my plans, whenever possible, involved my daughter. She was my adventurous child who was willing to experience anything placed before her. We would plan outings together such as trips to the hairdresser, to the nail salon, and to the dressmaker for our matching clothes. Trips to the ice cream parlor and restaurants for extravagant food always topped our list.

After a great meal out, we would attempt to recreate the dish we had devoured. She was always my willing tester. She was my young, fun-loving, ready-to-go, inquisitive amigo!

With her diagnosis, my role was changed to an unlicensed nurse. My daughter had diabetes, and it was my job to ensure that nothing bad happened to her. In doing so, I changed the way I cooked and shopped. I read every label to ensure the food was appropriate. I even bought a scale to weigh her food. Even though I was doing everything right, that absurd statement made by the social worker was ringing in the back of my mind. No one was going to take my baby girl!

At her school, I had a mini fridge added to her classroom to store her insulin and her emergency snacks. For any activities outside our home, I collaborated with the host to ensure that my daughter would be accommodated without her feeling different.

What I did not notice during this time was that my baby girl was drowning and missing our previous mommy-and-me relationship. She just wanted her fun mommy back.

I receive true revelation when I visited her at college for the first time. I saw glimpses of Ashley before her diagnosis. She was experiencing more than managing her blood sugar levels—engaging in many activities, living life to the fullest. Both the faculty and the students were expressing how full of life she was, and here I was merely focused on keeping her from death.

I went to my car and cried. God, why can't I enjoy my child? What happened? Where did my childhood dream go?

I wanted her healed and back to normal, but I had no power over that. Only God can perform that miracle. I had a decision to make: I could continue in my ways or embrace living with a child with type 1 diabetes.

I made a decision on that day to relinquish control and embrace the truth found in Romans 8:28 (KJV): "And we know that all things work together for good to them that love God, to them who are the called according to his purpose." It did not say all things would be good.

My daughter also solidified my decision with her wise words one day: "Mommy, I have type 1 diabetes, but type 1 diabetes does not have me."

That decision changed the dynamics of our relationship and returned it to the dream I had had as a child. In essence, I had to rely on God to guide both my daughter and myself through this process. And on days when it gets hard, I call to mind what my little girl said in the hospital: "Mommy, we will just have to make the best of this." Those words have stayed with me ever since. I have called them a standard to live by. Arise!

CONNECT WITH LEOLENE HINDS

 @leolenehindsim
 @leolenehinds & @lhiministries

Quick and in a Hurry

By Dr. Dorissa McCalister

"But Jesus immediately said to them: 'Take courage! It is I. Don't be afraid.'"
— Matthew 14:27 (NIV)

Is it funny that I think of God as my own personal superhero? Ready to save the day at a moment's notice? Able to create something from nothing, part entire seas, hold back the wind with His bare hands while simultaneously shielding me from hurt, harm and danger?

For as long as I can remember, I have believed that God is God, and that Jesus Christ is His only son and my Savior. I can't ever remember a time believing anything different.

I grew up in a household where faith and the gospel were like residents—familiar, loved, and constant—and of all the lessons I learned in my parents' home, the most important lesson I'll never forget is, "Faith and fear cannot coexist in the same space."

Using their lives as examples, both of my amazing parents taught my sister and me not to panic and not to be afraid when trouble arise, and that no matter how impossible a situation looked, we were not to rely on our own understanding but to trust God and focus on Him no matter what was happening around us.

Some may say we were sheltered and given unrealistic tools to cope with life's problems, but I beg to differ. I believe my faith-based upbringing and beliefs have served me well throughout the years.

In my younger years (I'm now fifty-seven), when trouble came my way and I couldn't, for the life of me, figure out the solution to what seemed to be an impossible problem, my knee-jerk reaction was to pray to God for help, and to believe He would come to my rescue faster than it took me to say, "Help me!"

Every time I called on Him, He answered...quick and in a hurry.

In elementary school, I was bullied by the neighborhood "mean girl," and I remember pleading to God to help me, and just like that, He did...quick and in a hurry.

When I was attending college in my twenties, carrying lots of angry inside of me (mostly because of my daddy's murder), I found myself making bad decisions, in bad relationships, and in bad situations that I couldn't get out of, but I'd call on God to help me, and time after time He did...quick and in a hurry.

Quick and in a hurry...isn't that how God operates?

One of my favorite Bible stories is about Peter and his cry for help.

Jesus instructed the disciples to get in their boat, cross the Sea of Galilee, and meet Him on the other side.

As the disciples crossed the sea, a sudden and frightening storm arose. The winds raged, and the waves tossed high, as the sky was overshadowed with darkness. I imagine they were afraid and convinced they were about to die.

Suddenly, a figure appeared walking toward them on the sea. Oddly, the disciples did not recognize Jesus, even though He had been their "friend" for a long time. Jesus made himself known by saying, "Take courage! It is I. Don't be afraid."

Peter, the impulsive one out of the twelve disciples, the one I am convinced is a distant relative of mine, instinctively and confidently answers, "Lord if it's you,... tell me to come to you on the water" (Matthew 14:28 NIV).

In faith, while staring at Jesus, Peter steps out of the boat and walks on water. He did fine—that is, until he took his eyes off Jesus and started paying more attention to the howling winds and raging waters around him.

His faith turned into fear.

He began to sink.

In just a few seconds, Peter had forgotten all that he had witnessed, experienced, and learned with Jesus in the past three years.

As Peter began to sink, he cried out, "Lord, save me!" (Matthew 14:30 NIV), and immediately, Jesus reached out His hand to rescue Peter. He then said to Peter, "You of little faith,...why did you doubt?"

Hmm...why did Peter doubt?

In my lifetime, I have experienced many storms: molestation, rape, mental abuse, physical abuse, divorce, bankruptcy, rejection, a mother with Alzheimer's, the murder of my father, and way too many deaths of close friends and family to count. And recently, as I've cried out to God for help, instead of His usual response of immediate rescue...

There's silence.

A silence so still, it pierces your heart.

A silence followed by many questions, while looking toward heaven and yelling at the top of my lungs, "God, don't you care about me?" and "I thought you said you'd never leave or forsake me? So, where are you?"

Just a few years ago, my faith—and my fear—were put on display just like Peter's. A storm arose. The storm's name was *homelessness*.

My mother had just passed from Alzheimer's, and my landlords had advised me that my daughter and I had to move because they had decided to sell their house. I suddenly had only sixty days to bury my mother, pack up our entire house, and find somewhere new to live.

What I thought would be a quick move turned into one week short of a year of homelessness.

Overnight, it seemed like everything, and everybody was conspiring against me.

Everything I tried, every favor I called in, and every trick in my there's-an-answer-in-here-somewhere book turned into an epic failure.

If a house listing posted at noon, and I called to inquire about it just ten or fifteen minutes later, I was told every time, there were already several people ahead of me on the waiting list.

My money was running low. My once near-perfect credit score was plummeting dangerously low because of the repetitive pulling of my credit.

Although we were able to secure a tiny place to lay our head (a far cry from the four-thousand-square-foot home we used to have), I couldn't help but feel like a failure because I couldn't "make it happen" and because I couldn't give my child a decent place to call home.

My faith was dwindling with every passing day...358 days, to be exact.

The overwhelming feelings of failure soon turned into anger, then fear.

I became so afraid. I could barely wake up every day. I was too afraid to even try. I cried all day and night. My fear paralyzed me to the point I couldn't provide for my daughter the way I desired and the way she deserved.

Every day I became increasingly afraid that God had abandoned me and had left me to fend for myself.

"HELLLP! God, where are you?"

I was sinking, and I was sinking fast in what felt like an eternal abyss. Each passing day grew darker. I felt like my life was out of control. Feelings of despair and hopelessness were starting to take over my thoughts. Fear had me gasping for air. I felt like I was drowning...like Peter.

Like Peter, as my fear increased, my faith decreased. I allowed myself to live in this stormy state of mind for a year...what was I thinking?

My perception needed to change. I needed to see my setback as a setup for my comeback.

I needed to lean into the teachings of my parents and remember what I had learned and lived my entire life—that God was always with me, that He would always come to my rescue, and that my faith should always be bigger than my fears.

As soon as I made the decision not to doubt, God rescued me. He literally answered my cry for help the moment I let go of my fear.

On the morning of day 358, my phone rang, and on the phone was a real estate agent, informing me that the four people ahead of me on the waiting list had all been disqualified for a house. I was able to schedule a walk-through that day and later received the keys to a brand new, never-been-lived-in house!

I remember crossing the threshold of the front door for the very first time and smelling that "new house" smell. I also vividly remember what came next.

The realtor handed me the keys and said, "Congratulations. The house just cleared inspections yesterday."

Yesterday? I thought.

I stood in my new kitchen, and a piece of protective plastic that was still on the oven door caught my eye. It was then that I heard God whisper to me, *"Daughter, why did you doubt? I never left you. I was with you and in control the entire time. I had to make you wait so you could learn to trust me. I couldn't give this house to you before today because I was still building it."*

Ashamed, I broke down in tears, repenting for my doubt. I wonder if Peter did the same.

I'm thankful that even when it feels like He's not showing up when and how I think He should, He always works it out for my good...quick and in a hurry.

CONNECT WITH DR. DORISSA MCCALISTER

 @IamDorissa

 @IamDorissa

 @dorissa

Goin' Up Yonder
By Dr. Felice Kelly Gillum

"We are confident, yes, well pleased rather to be absent from the body and to be present with the Lord."
—2 Corinthians 5:8 (NKJV)

If I close my eyes in a silent room, it seems like it was only yesterday. It's hard to believe it was nearly forty years ago that I had my first experience with death. I was in the second grade and didn't completely understand what was taking place. I remember my mother telling me that death was a normal part of life. That everyone must die at some point, and it was nothing to be afraid of.

When my great-grandmother passed away, I really didn't understand the level of anxiety and uncertainty that would come with attending her funeral services. I remember wanting to disappear into thin air because I was so uncomfortable. I sat with my favorite older cousin. I recall a line of people walking up to view my great-grandmother in a casket; as it was explained to me, this was your final resting place so they can bury you in the ground. It was all very overwhelming. Then I remember it came time for our row to go and view the body, and I didn't want any part of that. My cousin told me that I had to go. That I needed to see her one last time. So, I did. But I sure didn't like the feeling that came when I did.

My following funeral came shortly after. It was my paternal grandfather. That was strange because I didn't view him as a scary mythical creature as I did my great-grandmother. My granddaddy was funny, and he always made me laugh. He played games with us kids, and I loved every minute of it. We used to fight over who would push him in his wheelchair, and he never seemed to mind. He just went with the flow and was never loud or angry. So when I found out he had died, I was sad. I went and told my second-grade teacher and my class. They prayed for me as I cried. That was a tough pill to swallow for my seven-year-old self. His funeral was very different from my great-grandmother's. People were weeping and visibly sad. I can remember my cousin, who is also my best friend, passing out at the funeral and being taken out by one of the older deacons of the church. She and I were the same age. *What on earth was she passing out for?* I wondered. The whole experience was again very overwhelming, just on a different scale.

My next close experience with death came many years later, and it was one I could never have prepared for. I was in the eleventh grade, and one of my very first childhood friends, who was like a brother to me, passed away in an automobile accident. I wasn't quite sure how to process that. He passed on Good Friday in 1994. Shortly before then, a local basketball celebrity in our town had passed away. They held her services at our high school, and I remember they dismissed school early that day. I can still recall Roy telling me that day that the school would be closed the entire day when he passed away because he was so special, that it would be deemed a holiday. He was a little arrogant like that sometimes. I shook my head and told him to shut up. However, in just a few short weeks his prophecy was fulfilled, and he was correct. There was no school that day.

If there is such a thing as mourning yourself crazy, I'm sure that's what I did. I remember having so many thoughts going through my mind that I couldn't make sense of. I never wanted to drive again out of fear. I wished I had been in the car with him, so maybe we could have died together. I remember my mother finding a note that I wrote to him saying as much. She thought I was crazy and suicidal. I wasn't. I was a lost child trying to find her way in a world I no longer understood. I've realized since that after that experience, I probably needed therapy to help me process my emotions. Since I didn't receive it, I began to look at death much differently than I once had. It was like the glass was broken entirely and just left on the floor to step on repeatedly without healing the wound before.

Much later in my life, the year 2013 was when sickness and death reigned over me like a plague. It's certainly a year that changed my life forever. For years I had prayed for God to bless me with a son, and that year he did. However, I also went into heart failure while in labor and delivery and nearly lost my life. The thought of processing your own mortality brings a plethora of emotions. For me, the idea of leaving my family behind was almost unbearable. Although I came to peace with dying, I truly believed that my work on earth was not complete. I fought as hard as I could mentally and physically to go home to my family. Thankfully, God granted me that request and has since blessed me with an enriching life with my family. However, it took years for me to process the emotions associated with coming that close to death. To be honest, I am still processing them.

In the summer of 2013, I also lost the person who undoubtedly had the most significant impact on my life besides my parents. My beloved late pastor, Dr. Lewis E. Ragins Sr., was the closest thing to God that I knew here on earth. I could speak all day about Pastor Ragins—his love for God, family, church, community, and friends. He was the one I went to with the most significant struggles of my life. His guidance caused me to realign my life according to the Word, and that's when everything changed. I was so excited to introduce Pastor Ragins to our new son, Dallas. The last thing he told me when he saw my son was that Dallas was a blessing from God. At that moment, I knew he was proud of me for honoring God by returning to the spiritual foundation he set for me many years ago.

Pastor Ragins left us in July of 2013, and my Uncle, L. C., also transitioned in August of that same year. The following year my two favorite aunts passed away. Both had the most enormous hearts I have ever experienced in a woman. When I got pregnant with my daughter as a sophomore in college, Aunt Shirley wanted to move back home to Mississippi to help take care of my baby so I could return to college. No sacrifice was too great for the ones she loved. She understood me as I did her. I told her she had her own family to care for, and I would be just fine, and I was. Aunt Shirley passed in December of 2014. The same month we found out Aunt Diane had breast cancer. She left us in March of 2015. Someone once told me that I was just like my Aunt Diane. That I was too quick to run to the aid of everyone else and never put myself first. They said it as if they pitied me. I could not have been prouder.

I didn't deal well with the deaths of Pastor Ragins, Uncle L. C., Aunt Shirley, and Aunt Diane. I chose to take my mind and focus to a different place. It wasn't healthy, I knew that. But the thought of so much loss was too much to process.

I kept myself extremely busy with work and being a mom for the next few years. I had two beautiful biological children and three children to whom my husband and I had opened our home. My mourning process did not begin until I transitioned my sweet foster daughter out of the home after three years of loving her as my own. At that time, I mourned the loss of her so deeply. The grief was overwhelming, and it brought to the surface all the suffering for the others I had lost. And then my mind went completely blank. I had never been to that place in my mind before. It was a scary and unrecognizable place. My pain and grief became unbearable. I guess God just temporarily shut me down.

Through this entire experience, I have since learned that we must deal with grief as it comes to us. There are five stages of grief, and it's imperative to move through them all:

Stage 1: Denial

Stage 2: Anger

Stage 3: Bargaining

Stage 4: Depression

Stage 5: Acceptance

When we follow the appropriate stages of grief, we can get to a place of acceptance in a healthier way. After my dark, blank moment, I received the proper therapy I needed to return to a balanced frame of mind. I am now able to properly grieve the loss of my loved ones. My dad had two more sisters, to whom I was extremely close, who died. Although each process of grieving has been sometimes overwhelming, I also can laugh and remember the good times. It's a blessing to thrive on the beautiful memories of yesterday. Doing so in a healthy manner gives us such beautiful hope and promise for tomorrow.

If you or someone you know needs assistance processing the loss of a loved one, help is available to you. Please visit www.mhanational.org or schedule some time to talk with your medical professional about your feelings.

Through my journey I have grown spiritually and become more in tune with who I am and what I want out of life for the brief time that we have here on this earth. Revisiting thoughts of grief and mourning can be extremely overwhelming. I know this because even after writing this chapter, I am still processing the amount of grief incurred from losing my loved ones. However, one thing I know for certain is that God has prepared a place for His children after our life on Earth concludes. And for that I am most grateful.

CONNECT WITH DR. FELICE KELLY GILLUM

f @kellygirl0520

◎ @simply_felice

in @felice-kelly-gillum-a10a3754/

✉ belight@felicekellugillum.com

Arise and Walk by Faith in Real Time!
By Jean Turner

"An imbalance in any area of our lives creates imbalance throughout our entire being!"
—Jean Turner

Wherever you are in life, stop for a moment and imagine what it would feel like if suddenly, in the blink of an eye, your life was interrupted! Imagine what it would be like to suddenly find yourself in uncomfortable, unfamiliar territory. No longer "business as usual"! Now you are the one who everyone else turns to during troubled times. The "strong one"! Never let them see you sweat, right? But unbeknownst to everyone on the outside looking in, you are in a state of despair, currently in the fight of your life, and just fighting to stay alive so you can live to see another day!

The year was 2018. I was in the prime of my life, and I was beginning to see my retirement from the military on the horizon! I was a career girl in a man's world, a world where women were breaking barriers, creating their own paths, and doing some amazing things despite the "good ole boys club" mentality that resides withing the ranks of our nation's military. Then one day, I went from being the "strong one" to the one who needed someone, anyone, to be strong for me! Suddenly! Girl, interrupted! In one moment, I went from being this healthy army chick and marathon runner to cancer patient undergoing surgery, chemotherapy, congestive heart failure (due to the chemotherapy), dying in the emergency room, and fighting my way back from all of that to where God has me now in 2022: Healed, Healthy, and Whole!

As a thirty-five-year healthcare professional (an RN) who's always been healthy, never sick a day in her life (except for the occasional sinus infection or common cold), I suddenly found myself amid a healthcare crisis. Never in a million years did I imagine that would be me laying up in someone's intensive care unit. Never did I imagine I would lose all muscle strength in my legs and be in a wheelchair. I never thought I'd be the one needing physical and occupational therapy twice a day, seven days a week for almost two weeks so that I could rise from my sickbed and walk again!

My medical team told my family that I had a 1 percent chance of surviving. When I came out of my comatose state, some of these same providers said I would have to be on a machine for the rest of my life. There is a scripture that I meditated on often during this time in my life. It says, "Now faith is confidence in what we hope for and assurance about what we do not see" (Hebrews 11:1 NIV). I am a witness that whatever it is you are hoping for, it requires faith in the present moment. Faith during the actual event, situation, circumstance that is taking place. As I walked through the valley of the shadow of death, I envisioned myself running again. I told my family and my medical team, "I will run again!" Faith in the present moment gives life to the very thing you are hoping for.

What if my family and I believed what the providers said about my condition at that time?

What if my family and I believed what they predicted about my future?

What if I had chosen to believe their prognosis instead of believing the report of the Lord?

The medical team looked at my lifeless body and said to my family, "She's not going to survive the next few hours." Based on what they saw with their eyes and their medical knowledge and expertise, I was supposed to die. Thank God for family and friends who did not base the situation on what they saw in the natural. Instead, they chose to believe and speak life over my lifeless body. My boisterous, no-nonsense ninety-year-old auntie told the doctors, "She is not going to need to be on no machine at home! No! She is not going to need a permanent pacemaker! Jean is going to be all right!" All of them believed they would see the physical manifestation of what they were hoping for!

"Faith is the substance of ..." (Hebrews 11:1 KJV).

What does your faith consist of? Does it consist of confidence and trust in the Creator? A right-now faith, in other words, faith in real time, says that now, in this present moment, as I walk through this situation, I am confident that what I hope for will come to pass and the promise, the guarantee, though I don't see it now, will manifest in my future! Faith in real time says I look to Him with anticipation and expectation because I know He is working it all out for my good. Something good is going to come out of this adversity!

Say to yourself what apostle Paul says in 2 Corinthians 4:13 (NIV), "I believed; therefore, I have spoken." Faith in real time says, "I believe; therefore, I speak!"

Here we are—2022! I am grateful to God that I am doing everything the doctors said I would not do over three years ago, and I'm doing it free of machines, tubes, portable oxygen, assistive devices, etc. Even now, as you are reading my story, you may be reeling from the effects of a sickness, depression, an abusive relationship, a failed business or marriage, financial distress, anxiety, fear, trauma, or maybe something that is happening in real time. Whatever you are reeling from has you upset, confused, or maybe in a state of shock. Whatever it is has caused you to lose your balance. I totally get it!

If I may be transparent, there were days when I totally lost it! I asked the question, Why me? a gazillion times! I kept asking the question, What did I do to deserve this? Sometimes what we see as punishment is process! Yes, I had my days, some good and some not so good. Did my faith waver from time to time? Yes, it did! Were there times I allowed the situation to overtake me? Sure, but I didn't allow myself to stay in that place. I prayed and stayed in the Word. I meditated on scriptures of healing and on God's will for me to "prosper [be successful] in all things and be in health, just as [my] soul prospers" (3 John 1:2 NKJV). I remembered His plans for my life, to prosper me and to give me a future (Jeremiah 29:11)! I read, prayed, and meditated on the scriptures that let me know that what I was walking through at the time would all work together for my good because of my love for Him and because I am called for His purpose (Romans 8:28)!

Allow God's Word to penetrate and take up residence in your mind and heart. Mind-set matters, and because it matters, I knew I could not allow myself to stay in those dark places. Cry if you must, but do not allow yourself to stay in a dark place! Faith in real time requires that we be "transformed by the renewing of [your] mind" (Romans 12:2 NIV). It requires that we change our perspective, change how we think! I had the faith to believe and see myself healed and healthy again, but it required that I did something. We must do something. It takes faith and action to rise from our affliction (whatever that may be). It wasn't enough for me to believe. I had to arise, take up my bed, and walk, even when I was short of breath. I had to rest my body and get adequate sleep so that my body could heal and recover. Even when my husband and family wanted to cook for me, at some point I had to get up and begin doing it for myself. I had to be actively engaged in reversing my condition. I had to exercise my faith! Put my faith in forward motion!

Arise, take up your bed of affliction, and walk! Walk by faith in real time!

CONNECT WITH JEAN TURNER

🌐 www.spiritofawarrior.life

Rising from Brokenness

By Von M. Griggs

*"The most common way people give up their power
is by thinking they don't have any."*
—Alice Walker

After my military retirement, I'd recently relocated to Dallas, Texas, and had started on a new journey. I'd been in my new environment for all of eight months. Life was good and seemingly aligning with the plans God had for me. I was a divorced single mother of three children; my daughters were twenty-one and nineteen, and my son was twelve. This relocation was no harder than any other major move I'd experienced, except it was the very first time I was paying out of pocket to relocate my entire belongings. Up until then, the US Government Transportation Management Office took care of my moving expenses.

I'd been asked by a dear friend to come and assist her in her ministry expansion, as she was launching a new church. The move, along with having to search the territory and find a house and a school, was exciting, yet it came with some unwanted stresses and anxiety. My faith in God's leading was being stretched, because for the prior twenty years, someone else (i.e., the US Air Force) had decided where I would live and for how long. I closed my dry cleaning and safety and health consulting businesses and was on my way to experience the next transition on my life's journey.

Before arriving to live in Dallas, Texas, I had visited three times. I had conducted a reconnaissance, becoming familiar with the territory, the culture, etc., all to determine where I would purchase a home. My children were very excited to leave Mississippi. My daughters were both working in retail and secured jobs within the first three days of our arrival. My eldest daughter, a graduated licensed massage therapist, also began gaining new clientele in holistic body care. I was able to focus on doing nothing other than being Mom, as this was the first season in my life where I was not working full-time, so it was a much needed mental and physical slowdown.

I'd signed an agreement with Century 21 Real Estate Management under a lease to purchase. After my twelve-month lease, my funds would be attributed to the 20 percent required down payment, or so I thought.

After starting a new position, I was away traveling for work when I was notified by my youngest daughter that "a man in a white car and suit had rung our doorbell and left a business card on the door." I returned home a few days later and noticed the business card on the stack of unread mail, yet I thought it was no more than a solicitation. This was during the times of moving into a new community and receiving a welcome basket filled with advertisements, coupons, and the like. Regrettably, three weeks later, I beat myself down for not having responded to that business card. I was being evicted with a thirty-day grace period to relocate. The property was in a foreclosure, and I was illegally trespassing. My newly hired real estate attorney informed me of Texas law and, without empathy, said there was no legal ground for me to stand on. After all, Century 21 was a reputable real estate management company. Did my agent not know the laws? I was furious, angry, and overwhelmed with panic and fear over what to do next.

Brokenness set in, and I felt so distraught, I couldn't even accept that I was now facing being unhoused. It was the first time in my life I was not able to provide a safe place for my children. God, what was happening? Had I missed Him? Should I have remained in Mississippi? I could barely sleep for weeks, leading up to our departure from the residence that had been illegally leased to us. My identity was broken because I was no longer the provider my children needed. I prayed drastically for quick answers and resources.

As far as I knew, I'd done everything right. I was a dual-property owner with my first residential property being in the United Kingdom; however, it had been vacant for five months and I was paying that monthly mortgage as well. I'd never, ever been in a situation like this. My parents had always provided shelter for me, and so had the US Air Force. I had no reference point, no comparison even to consider.

Ten days before my required departure date, Hurricane Katrina hit the Mississippi Gulf Coast, damaging my second property, forcing my tenants to be reassigned to another out-of-state military base. Now I had two vacant properties to keep mortgages current and I was searching for another resident. I remembered God's promise that He would always "perfect that which concerns me" (Psalms 138:8 NKJV).

Being evicted was very humiliating because when I reached out to people for assistance, I was questioned and scrutinized with their judgmental questions. I remember one lady telling me, "You have too much." Really?! I was making the American Dream manifest for me. After all, I was the first of my siblings to purchase two homes. Wasn't I supposed to surpass my parents' achievements who were illiterate in formal education and raised us during the Jim Crow era? Had I achieved too much? Had pride become a factor in this progress? I was a divorced single parent of three children and a six-month-old granddaughter. What I thought were achievements, I would soon learn others saw with envy. My spirit was broken when I had to humble myself and seek resources that were very foreign to me. *But God!*

I went from agency to agency, being told "no" more times that I can remember. This rejection was continually breaking me down. The humiliation of completing pages of applications only to have representatives of the agencies tell me they could not help. I had assets, and they could not assist me if I had *any* income. I was receiving my military retirement pay and working at the Dallas VA Medical Center. I was told to sell my car and furnishings that were in a storage facility.

This is when I became aware of inequalities as a veteran and a single mother with children. I soon witnessed that housing was only provided for veterans who are single but not with families. What an epiphany and equally a disgrace. Who were these people to deny me? Is this the great country that I'd dedicated and sacrificed to serve? I even had a lady tell me, "I was a lucky dog to have lived overseas," since she had never lived outside of the state. I had become so naked and vulnerable while broken down and in despair.

Finally, God led me to one facility on a Saturday morning. I told the receptionist I would not complete any papers, but she said she would listen to me, and if she could help me, then I would need to reveal my personal information. Listen she did. Then she prayed with me. She *bent* the requirements, told me exactly what to put on the intake forms. After reviewing their policies with me, she informed me that due to the ages and genders of my youngest daughter and son, she could not provide for all of us. The decision was made for my son and youngest daughter to reside with my oldest daughter, as she had secured an apartment by then. Even that was a risk due to housing authority regulations, which didn't allow that number of occupants in a two-bedroom apartment. *But God!*

It was hilarious to me when I realized that some of the ladies I lived with at the homeless sheltered thought I was an undercover vice officer. While they stayed away from me as much as much as possible, I knew they were watching me and talking about me. I was broken to receive no embrace or acceptance from them, yet I had faith that God would provide, even though He appeared to be silent.

Finally, during a Saturday morning breakfast in the cafeteria, one of them came over and sat with me. She bravely started to tell me of her drug addiction, how she had abandoned her children, leading up to asking me why I was there. She told me it was obvious I did not belong with them. I was driving a Jaguar and kept my clothing neatly folded in the trunk, because remember, I wasn't supposed to have any assets. Taking anything of value into the facility was risky due to theft and who I was sharing the space with.

Fortunately, I had joined the Texas State Guard, and during Hurricane Katrina, my unit, now in Dallas, Texas, had been given military orders for six months, effective immediately. I was serving as a second lieutenant in the command post as a Shelter Manager. My stay in the shelter was three weeks, as the state officials assigned us to hotels. I transitioned from shelter status to a suite in Dallas's historic Hotel Lawrence. I now had three incomes, and I was slowly regaining a grip on my life while serving evacuees from Louisiana. I could understand and pray with many of them because I empathized with their dilemmas.

This is when I made a vow to God that when I rose up from this life-altering situation, I would be an advocate for unhoused female veterans with children, without judgment and partiality.

CONNECT WITH VON M. GRIGGS

[f] @VonMGriggs

[◎] @joyrestoredoutreach

[⊕] www.griggsenterprise.net & www.joyrestoredoutreach.org

Arise & **SHINE**

Be Relentless!
By Nicole D. Roberts

*"Put Jesus and His Kingdom over and above everything
and never stop praying!"*
—Nicole D. Roberts

I had heard the voice of God calling me to feed His people with the truth, and I thought all the negative things: that I am not good enough and that maybe it wasn't really God's voice I heard. I told my mother, and she said to do what God says. I should have thought her affirmation was enough; it wasn't. I called the prayer line, and the person on the other end of the telephone advised me to come speak to a senior team member for guidance and direction. I made an appointment, and when I got there, I had to explain who I was, why I had come, and what was I looking for. When I told the prayer line counselor I had written a book, he asked, "Do you know how to write a book?" I pushed past the negativity and shared with the counselor my vision to have a conference. I told him that it had come to me in a dream. I thought I needed to be honest, open, and transparent about my visit and why I needed help and direction. I asked whether or not I should leave my job and follow the vision God had given me. I was expecting some constructive feedback filled with hope and love, but what I received was a total put-down, being told that I am not good enough, being told I am a nobody and if I had a conference, no one would come and lots of other negative comments. I felt like I had just gone back to the pit that I just fought to come out of. I felt hopeless and wanted to give up. I continued to sit down and listen to this person put me down and make me feel worthless. Then it was over, and I left their office and walked to the car with my head down, my dreams destroyed. I started crying and bawling in the car because I felt so hopeless and so destroyed by this person that I thought I would give up. I felt lost!

The problem was I had told the wrong person about my dreams, vision, and calling. I had faith in the wrong person, thinking that when I went to them, they would cheer me on and support the fact that I wanted to follow God with all my heart, soul, and mind. I chose to ask a human about something that was about God, something spiritual. In this I had made a big mistake. I had not expected someone that I looked up to for advice and guidance would speak to me with such rejection, intimidation, disrespect, and dishonor and make me feel like garbage (putting it nicely).

So, I sat in my car and cried. But then I carried on and went home feeling sad and hopeless. My son asked me why I was crying. I told him part of the experience, and he replied, "Jehovah has the final say!" My son brought the light back, and I continued sharing the Word as I was called to on different platforms in my books with the goal of reaching one soul per day.

There are some women and men in a position of power for the wrong reasons. They may have fallen by the wayside, and they project a different mask when in public than in private. Who they are in the public eye on a stage, "demons in disguise," is different from who they are behind closed doors. Just because they are in a position of power or influence does not mean they want you to succeed or move forward. Remember, this person is a mere human being, and they can also kill, steal, and destroy your dreams, vision, or calling. Hold on to the kingdom assignment God has given you. Become like the children of Israel when they were walking around the walls of Jericho. When the vision has materialized and manifested, let it be your testimony. Do not speak to anyone; just give shouts of praise to God.

You can use the strategies I've learned in order to live empowered. I have learned that this type of situation is practice, which means it is preparation for what is coming ahead. There are valuable lessons to learn, and by missing them, you will be unprepared for the next challenge. When someone does this sort of thing to you, do not hate them, for they are playing their part in preparing you for the war. Your situation is equipping and empowering you to continue to rise above challenges. You are being tested; testimony comes after! You have to keep doing what God has called you to do, no matter how small the difference you are making. Stay obedient to God's calling and His work. God sees your faithfulness and obedience, and He rewards those who diligently seek Him. Do not leave your church because someone offended you; stay there and win the war because the battle belongs to the Lord. Church prepares you for every challenge. The people in the church are the same as in the world, and yes, they should be different, but stay focused, keep your eyes on Jesus, keep serving in church, and keep going to church for the Word of God never fails. Focus on the Word, not on the war!

Remember who God is, your Creator, your heavenly Father, your best friend, and the one who is faithful *forever*!

If you cannot remember this, take some time to study the Word and find out. *Know who God is for yourself.* Know who you are in Christ. Find out how God sees you, what your identity and worth are in Him!

Pray for those who offend you.

Forgive those who offend you.

Love those who offend you always, and never speak bitter words about them. Remember, they are God's children too.

Try to take your eyes off the hurt quickly and see the hope of your calling, see Jesus, the Great Physician, the one who heals all our disease and all our pain.

Do not let anyone stop you from doing the work of God.

Show up! Show up! Show up!

My hope is to encourage more people to become representatives of Christ. You may not want to be in the spotlight, but because you heard God's voice, tell the next person about Jesus and what He has done in your life. Tell one person, start there.

I want more people to win souls for Jesus.

I want to encourage the person reading this to believe in yourself.

Love God always and love yourself too!

Even in the middle of the tests and tribulations, never stop pursuing God first, never stop praying globally, never stop praising God, and never stop pressing toward the goal, the prize God has promised you. Philippians 3:14 (NLT) says, "I press on to reach the end of the race and receive the heavenly prize for which God, through Christ Jesus, is calling us."

Be inspired to rise and shine for God's glory every day!

CONNECT WITH NICOLE D. ROBERTS

f @authornicoledroberts

⊙ @nicoledroberts9639

🌐 www.nspglobal.co.uk

Overcomers — Reborn by Faith

By Dr. Judy Ambrose James

"Trust in the LORD with all your heart and lean not on your own
understanding; in all your ways submit to him,
and he will make your paths straight."
—Proverbs 3:5–6 (NIV)

Let me start this with some real solid advice. Identify with people who make the most out of their lives. When you are given a second chance at life, do not waste it by asking, why me? Take life one amazing day at a time. If you have never had a near-death experience, I don't expect you to appreciate where I am coming from. For the many of you who have, there is no time like the present.

Attention, overcomers! I have a message for you today! We know by experience that tomorrow is not promised. We must see life beyond disability and visualize a future with no pain, no cane, no brace, and no more days of rehab.

Where is all this wisdom and dreaming coming from? Well, in short, I had a stroke. Before my stroke, I tried to be all things to all people, to my family, friends, employer, even the dog. I thought all family problems needed to be solve by me, and I tried wearing every hat with a warped sense of pride. If I could not solve the problem, I would wear myself out trying. The stroke was a harsh wake-up call, forcing me to accept the realization that only God can be all things to all people.

I have been reborn by faith. I never understood what people meant by the expression "Keep the faith"—that is, until my stroke. "Now faith is the substance of things hoped for, the evidence of things not seen" (Hebrews 11:1 NKJV). By grace God can move mountains of doubt, worry, confusion, stress, fear, and lack. These scriptures are the underpinning of my life. It has been a long time coming, but there's been a major change in me. Everything I have been worried about, I put on the altar—my health, bills, children, enemies, etc. I honestly have no worries today in comparison to my life pre-stroke.

Let me give you a peek into my day-to-day life. The burning pain in my right foot is unimaginable, and no manufactured drug can ease it. I have called out to Jesus, like the woman with the issue of blood for twelve years. Ironically, it has been twelve years for me also. I truly feel if I can get close enough to touch the hem of His garment, I will be healed too.

He is Spirit; therefore, wherever I am, He is there.

This is why I continue to pray for an abundance of relief. I tried rubbing my right foot into submission, but spasticity and the burning had control. I was told repeatedly, by the many physical therapists I have had the pleasure of working with throughout fourteen years of rehab, that it was normal with some strokes. There is nothing normal about this pain. If I hear the words *normal pain* again, I will pull out what is left of my hair. I know there are stroke overcomers out there who can relate, those crippled mentally or physically by an affliction of the nervous system.

Because of my weakened immune system, I have had shingles six times. Yes, six! Have you ever seen the commercial describing the burning of the body from shingles, and did it make you cringe? Can you imagine experiencing this six times? Even after the vaccine, the virus returned. If you can identify with any of this, I need you to know that you are not alone in your pain - no matter how normal the professionals say your pain is. It has given me no choice but to hold on to my faith.

There are days when I sit on the bed, legs crossed, and suddenly my right foot involuntarily starts to flex uncontrollably. I reach down to grab hold of my right ankle, recognizing the flexion and knowing exactly what to do to stop it. I deep rub the swelling until it surrenders, and then elevate my right leg. My physical therapists have helped me understand how to combat these issues. Over the years, they have helped me see that with consistent exercise, my nervous system will improve, and that impacts my heart health for the better as well.

After each episode of foot flexion I had, a nightmare would follow that evening. During most of these, thank God, I did not remember the details. The ones where I did remember the details took me back to the night of my stroke, and I asked God to put a hedge of protection around me. It still seemed like the devil was always waiting in the wings for his opportunity. I had sinned minutes before the stroke, and God knew I would sin in the future. I asked for His forgiveness, acknowledging Jesus as my Lord and Savior, past, present, and future. Because of God's unconditional love, I received the miracle of His forgiveness. The devil left with his tail tucked between his legs again. Thank you, Jesus!

As I look back, my healing journey has been filled with highs and lows. Something as simple as going up the stairs to pick up my granddaughter without assistance and failing would steal my joy. It was on an evening right after a low point like this that I walked out of the house, headed down the street with no particular destination in mind. I was distraught and I did not want to talk to anyone. I desperately needed a win. My loved ones tried reassuring me that better days were coming. I struggled to see that far ahead. Where were the better days? I was so tired of chasing after them, I couldn't see the light for the darkness. Outrage did not begin to describe what I felt. Talk about an inner struggle! My spirit was saying, "For God has not given us a spirit of fear, but of power and of love and of a sound mind" (2 Timothy 1:7 NKJV), while on the other hand the fear of never walking with normalcy had taken its toll on me. I really had to dig deep and activate my faith! I had to remind myself regularly that nothing is impossible with God. *Even when the blows keep coming.*

Unfortunately, while healing from my stroke, I was stricken with another illness that wasn't immediately diagnosed and went untreated. Specifically, I would sometimes start laughing for no reason whatsoever. My family and I spent many years not realizing that my inappropriate giggling fits and lack of emotion (specifically crying) was a disease. I distinctly remember when my family members would try to make me laugh on purpose just so they could laugh at me.

Over time my spontaneous fits of laughter brought on stares and whispers from the ones I loved most. Eventually I was diagnosed in 2009. The medical term is called Pseudobulbar Affect (PBA). I can remember one day when my brother arrived at our house in distress. Turned out, he was having a heart attack. He was rushed to the hospital where we prayed and eventually lost him. Our entire family, including his daughter, was in shock. Naturally, they cried openly, but I couldn't shed one tear. The level of pain I was experiencing was excruciating on the inside, but outside—nothing!

When I finally ran out of explanations and excuses, I fell to my knees and begged God to please let me cry. Looking back, I'd experienced traumatic illness, depression, a broken heart, self-pity, and loss—the top reasons any normal person would cry. However, it wasn't until I asked God for help that my tears were released. Only God knew the hour of my miracle. I just had to believe. I am telling you all this so you will not sit around worrying about why your breakthrough has not happened yet. In His time, it will. So do not even think about giving up. Not if you want to live an empowered life. Please hear my heart and appreciate the advice.

I have come to learn that the imagination lends an interpretation of the world that makes sense. I am sure that anyone who has not experienced paralysis or any traumatic injury would dispute this way of thinking, even call it unhealthy. I would never recommend the imagination as the first line of defense for dealing with problems. Jesus said, "Seek ye first the kingdom of God, and his righteousness; and all these things shall be added unto you" (Matthew 6:33 KJV). Partner this with the fact that many therapists help their clients overcome traumatic moments by instructing them to "think of a happy memory or place." Well, that's what I'm saying: the only way you can walk again is to believe it and see it first. That is what I call radical faith! You can call it imagination if you like, but I know that partnering the word with radical faith is the reason I'm walking today. I had to see it and believe it first! So go ahead and live it up in your imagination, and then speak with the authority God has given you!

I believe the reason I am still alive is that I have something phenomenal to add to this world. Every contribution begins as a thought. Your ambitions and aspirations are in reach. Imagine. The sky's the limit.

There's no question, I am *reborn*. For the first time in my life, I *believe*. For the first time in my life, I am a *free spirit*. For the first time in my life, I am *powerful*. I have a reason to look forward to tomorrow. But if tomorrow does not come, I thank God He gave me today. I thank God for the people He has put in my life today. I thank God I can walk. I thank God I can talk. I thank God I am of sound mind and body. I thank God I can thank God.

CONNECT WITH JUDY AMBROSE JAMES

f @judyambrose.james

@judyambrosejames

Arise & **SHINE**

The Struggle in Me
By Sentretta Brumfield-Baity

*"Whoever dwells in the shelter of the Most High will rest
in the shadow of the Almighty. I will say of the LORD,
He is my refuge and my fortress, my God, in whom I trust."'*
—Psalms 91:1–2 (NIV)

My mom in a car crash thrown into a tree,

all the while not knowing she was pregnant with me.

Waking up months later to a decision to make,

my life or hers, which one would she take?

Well, nine months later and I'm still here,

thanks to a praying grandmother who knew with God on her side there was nothing to fear.

Into the world I came with a name from a joke she tells.

"Lord, I done sinned, we done hit a tree," and she began to stutter, "ta-ta-ta.",

A joke I didn't find funny, nor did I want to hear.

A little girl who lived in the hood,

with dope fiends, drug dealers, and people who meant no one any good.

A little girl who was innocent and full of life,

but the enemy was setting me up to steal my light.

As I continued to grow,

with dirty old men watching with their eyes all aglow.

A touch here, a feel there, with threats in their groans.

All I really wanted was for them to leave me alone.

Praying that the nightmares would go away,

the only one that would have protected me was gone to her grave.

Raping me as I cried and felt dirty inside,

Wishing there was somewhere that I could just hide,

and sometimes I felt that it would be okay if I just died.

Why? I would ask God and no answer came.

While those who were in authority turned a deaf ear and closed their eyes,

and as time went on, I would never be the same.

I began to build walls,

and a fire raged inside as my heart became hard and cold as ice.

Life was teaching me that some people just weren't nice.

Little did I know that through all the toil and strife,

God had a plan, and his hand was on my life.

This was only the beginning, I tell you; you will see,

just keep reading on, for the struggle is in me.

I'd already been in the storm, hell I was born in the storm.

I give up. Someone rescue me,

I might as well join the streets, let it be what it be.

God don't love me, and no one cares,

let me find my solace in what's out there.

How bad could it be? I'm already numb; what more could happen?

Boy, was I dumb!

Opening new doors feeding generational curses.

Throw the prayers out the window.

Listen, devil, I concede. How 'bout I don't serve you or God?

You started this war and God has the Bible verses.

Why do I have to be a part of your evil worship?

Leave me alone, go play chess by yourself,

I'll do just fine all by myself.

Three kids, a single mother trying to fit into the streets,

definitely headed for the land of defeat,

Never knowing that was not my destiny; I wasn't supposed to fit in.

Yet where was God when I needed him?

Defensive, nontrusting, just broken within.

Dealing with addiction to drugs, alcohol, rejection, and verbal abuse,

a sister like me struggling with what's right and juggling what's wrong,

Thank God I learned early how to be strong.

I knew God, but does He know me?

Homeless, bad relationships, where was my God through it all?

Did He forget about me?

Was my destiny in life to fail and fall?

I no longer trusted God, though I thought I did.

You see, He was my superhero there was nothing He couldn't see me through.

See, some of you could feel me through this because I am YOU!

Time after time I fought and I prayed through hurt and through pain,

and yet here I am still shackled in chains.

Church hurt, fake friends, people smiling in my face.

Lord, I'm going to lose my mind, I can't keep up with this pace.

Jail, divorce so I thought, young naive, used, abuse, rejected, and battered.

Lord, at this point even my armor is shattered.

No need for therapy; what was that going to change?

Lord, no one knows my inner pain.

Was I born to live a life of shame, alone and confused, with nothing to gain?

My story can go on, for there is so much to tell,

yet at this point I'm going to tell the devil to go to hell.

Take your misery, poverty, and strife.

I'm in therapy now, and I'm taking back my life.

You see, through it all there were decisions to make.

I took the wrong road as when in pain we often take.

I'm here to tell you, use your head and think,

The devil is deceitful in all his ways.

He plays with your mind and deals lethal blows.

It's his job to keep you from God goals.

Hold on tight to God's unchanging hand, never let go, He has a plan.

Trust in the Lord with all your might; it's not your battle, it's just your plight.

It started on the day you were born, your free will versus your evil will.

We already know the devil comes to steal.

He wants your anointing, your gift, your life.

He wants to fill your life with strife.

Your mind is his best playing field.

He moves through suggestion and bends your will.

He keeps throwing things at you and using his imps.

He uses the weak to build his strength.

He keeps hitting your armor until it is worn,

yet the Bible tells us the veil has been torn.

The next time your eyes are filled with tears,

remember, your mind has been filled with fears.

Take up your armor, your shield and sword.

Stand strong in the fight, for the battle is not yours.

God has already planned a way for you to escape.

Just remember, it's your will and your decision to make.

I had to remember and arise and shine,

And remembering that alone, I knew I would be just fine.

I'm walking in a new light now,

for everything that happened to me in life,

I had to remember and reflect within me.

I'm the one accountable to set myself free.

For everyone I looked to blame,

my mindset was wrong; my identity has now changed.

Victims will make victims, and they often do.

God does not break free will; you do what you must do.

I am no longer the victim of you and you and you.

You'll reap what you sow, yet I pray for you.

It is my due diligence to forgive you.

Some things I allowed due to low self-esteem,

yet now I know I am royalty, for I sit with the King.

My journey is not over. I have a ways to go,

yet this part of my life I have to let go.

Holding on only hurts me; the Holy Spirit came along and told me so.

"Let it be, my child, use wisdom; I give it to you for free."

"Yes, doors were open; let it go, let it be."

"It's not you versus them; it's your mind holding on that causes your plight."

"Forgive and move on; it's no longer your fight."

"How can I heal you if you're at war within?" He quietly said.

"It's your decision to win. Your words have power, so speak what will be."

"You cannot win a war that's not yours; you're a chosen child, don't you see?"

"It's you versus you now.

"You've made up enemies from the walls that you built,

and you stand now on the defense."

"Your mind is deceived from notions you conceived."

It was at that point I reflected on me,

and all the things that kept me from being free.

See, the struggle was no longer what happened to me.

I couldn't be healed I was holding on to rage,

and all of the things I chose to engage.

I was seeking sympathy from anyone, and yes,

all that happened was real indeed, yet I couldn't let go, I couldn't break free.

No, God didn't stop it, but He intervened.

I am alive and well; the devil couldn't have me.

I was suffering from post-traumatic stress, if it's an excuse you need,

yet I have free will too, and I choose not to let the devil succeed.

Satan has no power over anything.

Weapons may form against me, yet God's Word says

if I believe and just have faith the size of a mustard seed,

Satan's plan shall not prosper, and he stands in defeat.

I then understood it was no longer the enemy. The struggle was in me!

CONNECT WITH SENTRETTA BRUMFIELD-BAITY

f @synttbrumfield-baity

@ladysyntt & @beautybeyondskynn

beautybeyondskynn@gmail.com

Prepared for a Comeback

By Theresa F. Thompson

"God is our refuge and strength, an ever-present help in trouble."
—Psalm 46:1 (NIV)

"Theresa, Mom just got out of emergency surgery. They removed a grapefruit-sized mass from her colon."

Devastation took my breath, and I whimpered from the unexpected news my brother had just delivered. I pondered about leaving the military training I was attending, but I didn't want to return at a later date.

My mother was diagnosed with colon cancer days after the call. She was a super trooper battling the disease and still making an effort to work full-time. Despite the chemotherapy drugs treating her like a tackling dummy on a football field, God blessed her with the ability to praise Him through it all. I know that meditating on Bible verses and affirmations, taking bucket list trips, and spending quality time with friends and family were the key to her joy.

Five years of being optimistic came to an abrupt end with a frantic call from my mother: "I have stage 4 colon cancer. The doctors have given me the best drugs on the market."

My life was placed on hold, devastated all over again. I sat at my work desk and bawled my eyes out. A family member and I flew home to Wichita. I quickly got off the plane and drove straight to the oncology clinic. My mother was receiving her very last chemo treatment. Finally, my brothers arrived, and we met with her doctors and nurses for her final hospice preparations. It was determined I would the best caregiver for my mother. Within one week, we dismantled my mother's estate. My youngest brother and I drove my mother to my military quarters in Northern Chicago. We had the best daily visits until she was no longer able to function without heavy pain medication. My mother entered her new residence in heaven one sunny April afternoon.

Later, when I experienced my second great loss, I continued to question God about being my refuge and strength.

My loving husband, anchor, and best friend was my lifeline during the loss of my mother. We served together in the military.

My husband wasn't feeling well when he returned home from a family event, which I wasn't able to attend. I quickly stepped into the motherly role of getting him comfortable, fixing him a light meal, and doling out some meds. After a few days with no relief, I made sure he had an appointment with his doctor.

Once again, I got a call that rattled my world, this time sitting at my desk on a Friday afternoon. My husband's first call instructed me to meet him at Walter Reed Medical Center. Then a second call came with instructions to meet him at the emergency room at Fort Belvoir Community Hospital. I rushed over with a fear that was so familiar. Worry settled deep down in my bosom. I started praying for a miracle. After an unusually long wait, blood samples, X-rays, and an ultrasound, the doctors discovered a mass in my husband's stomach. Immediately, I saw something in his eyes that was unfamiliar: gut-wrenching fear.

Due to military installations being short-staffed on the weekends, my husband was released to go home with a follow-up appointment for an MRI the following Wednesday. The weekend was spent trying to be strong for one another, both paralyzed by the reality that sat before us. Neither one of us had an appetite. We notified both families with the news and asked for their prayers.

After we returned home from his appointment on Wednesday, my husband received a call from the gastroenterologist, calling with the results from the initial tests.

"By the way, I also have the results of your MRI from this morning. We usually don't give them over the phone, but you wouldn't be able to schedule an appointment until next week. If you are comfortable with it, I can share them with you now."

We looked at each other, thrilled to not have to wait. "Yes, we want to know now," my husband replied.

"The mass is pancreatic cancer."

We ended the call and cried. We sat still for hours, bewildered.

Then I sprang into action, becoming my husband's caregiver.

As we were navigating our new normal, tragedy hit again. I was performing a routine physical training test when I experienced a stroke. I was rushed to the hospital. When I saw my husband, I noticed that now familiar gut-wrenching fear in his eyes.

The tables had turned, and my husband soon became my caregiver. I was forever grateful. The days were long and painful, but God gave me strength during my recovery.

Soon I returned to the role as my husband's caregiver. We experienced months of both joy and pain. Visits to the hospital outside of regular chemo treatments increased. On our last visit to the emergency room, my husband was admitted. God allowed my loving husband to share his last birthday with family and friends by his bedside.

But God! He really is my refuge and strength. He ordered my steps during those precious last days.

The hospital staff allowed two separate days for family and friends to come say their last words to my husband while he still had a great presence of life. He was discharged and sent home on hospice and entered his new residence twenty-four hours later. I'm forever grateful for having the best husband who loved me unconditionally. "I miss you, hubby!"

I wonder, how can the fragile mind survive life's rigorous tests?

On the passing of my husband, I received a new revelation of God being my refuge and strength. Then I experienced an all-too-familiar pattern.

I was away on military business. I had just arrived at my hotel room after dinner and received an unexpected call from my father explaining that he had to undergo a surgical procedure on his bile duct. This was so upsetting to hear because my husband had had a similar experience; it brought all that back. I collapsed on the floor and sobbed for what seemed like an eternity. Two weeks later, I went running home to Kansas to be the hero of order.

My father was diagnosed with stage 4 gall bladder cancer days later during his surgery. Devastation took its toll at that point! It felt like a pin had dropped and burst a balloon on my life. I became a pro at being a caregiver. After months of chemo treatments, I decided that my military career was on its final leg, and it was very important for my father to be present for my retirement ceremony. It was my last gift to him, as proud as he was of his youngest daughter's achievements. My father got his wings early morning on December 4. The Lord prevails!

Let me tell you about the God I serve. He laid the groundwork me for my comeback four years later. I learned through grief that pain and joy can coexist. Initially, I ran from grieving as fast as a race car driver. Frankly, I just wanted to die and I thought I couldn't go on with life. Why? I lacked a small mustard seed type of faith.

It was during a visit to the oncology department, to deliver a token of appreciation, that my husband's therapist looked at me and knew I was clinically depressed and feeling hopeless after the loss of my husband. That same therapist became my mental health life coach. She saved my life. Thank God she was saved and filled with the Holy Ghost! Upon my move to Charlotte, I was blessed to find and also joined a widowed women's group with an extraordinary leader whom I know was sent by God! I also acquired a wonderful, beast-mode personal life coach whom I met through my church.

Through God's amazing handiwork and my faith in Him my love was shared, my joy was spread, and I have peace within my soul that was received by my loved ones. I'm living my best life!

As the saying goes, "Life is like riding a bicycle: to keep your balance, you must keep moving!"

CONNECT WITH THERESA F. THOMPSON

@chosenbeyond8

Arise & **SHINE**

One Decision Can Change Everything

By Shawn "Casey" Collins Jr.

"When everything seems to be going against you, remember that the airplane takes off against the wind, not with it."
—Henry Ford

I f you are reading this, you are in for a ride. I want to tell you a story about a kid with nine lives. Well, maybe not nine, but believe me, the envelope was pushed. This is a real-life story about a beautiful summer day when a little dude just wanted to play with his Transformers and Power Rangers. I was a typical four-year-old boy making my mom late by playing with my toys in the middle of the living room when I was supposed to be getting ready to leave for our appointment.

What I thought was going to be a cool day hanging out with my mommy and baby brother Na'im turned into one of the scariest days of my little four-year-old life. As we were leaving, my mom received a phone call that changed my life forever! My doctor's office called with the results of some blood tests that I had done recently. They told my mom that we needed to go to John Hopkins Hospital immediately. Innocently, she responded that we were on our way out to take some family portraits. She asked if we could go take our family pictures first or if we should head to the hospital right away. The response was immediate: "No, you've got to go right now!" So she cancelled the family portrait session, and we went directly to John Hopkins Hospital.

Who are these people and what is going on?

I didn't understand what was going on around me. When we arrived, my mom got the news that they thought that I had leukemia. They said they needed to do more testing to confirm the diagnosis. As they began, she called my dad, Tia Tonia, my grandma, and her closest friends and told them to meet us at the hospital. We spent the whole day doing tests and talking to doctors in the emergency room. There were needles and then more needles and more conversations with doctors. All I wanted was for them to stop. I remember telling my mommy, "Make them stop!" It was hurting me, and I didn't understand why they were doing this to me. Mom and Dad held my hand to make me feel better, but the needles just kept coming.

Now, as an adult, I can't even begin to imagine what my parents must have been going through, all while trying to figure out how to explain it all to me. I know they wished they could make it all go away for me. My mother wondered what she did wrong to cause this to happen. They had all kinds of questions running through their heads while trying to hold it together and be strong for me and each other. How did we get here? Why *our* baby boy? Our firstborn child. Family and friends came from everywhere: Chicago, Seattle, New York, and more. I recall seeing so many people crying in one place.

Mom said she was sorry but that I was sick. I remember thinking, *really? But I feel fine.* Ultimately, we did find out the official diagnosis. I was diagnosed with T-cell ALL, or acute lymphoblastic leukemia that day. My mom met Lesley, an amazing oncologist, who shared that the prognosis for my type of leukemia was usually successful with chemotherapy. With the right course of treatment, they expected me to do just fine. Best news of the day!

After we spent all day in the ER, they finally got me settled in and admitted to the intensive care unit. The next step was to do a procedure that would clean my blood so my body would accept chemotherapy. That would be followed immediately by chemo the next day. I was hooked up to so many tubes that it was hard for me to move! There were times my parents had to leave the room during a procedure. Those times were the scariest. My dad called me Champ (one of my nicknames), and he told my mom, "Our Champ will be okay."

What a day! We all just wanted to go home, but I wouldn't be leaving the hospital for a very long time. My mommy was very pregnant with a due date quickly approaching. As a precaution, the doctors decided they would save the cord blood, just in case it was needed for a cord blood transplant for me down the road. As timing would have it, the day took another incredible twist. My mom, undoubtedly stressed from the day's events, took what she thought was a normal trip to the bathroom, only to discover she was in labor. About forty-five minutes later my sister, Sydni, was born, just after midnight. They were able to save her cord blood as previously discussed. That decision ultimately saved my life. You better believe I felt sick and tired the next day, but the highlight of the day was when they brought my newborn sister to see me in the ICU. I was able to hold her just a few hours after her birth!

A few weeks into my treatment, we received an update that was not encouraging. I failed induction. That meant the chemotherapy was not working. They told my parents that I may only have nine months to live. They wanted to try an experimental treatment on me to stop the spread of the cancer, but they would also need to do a bone marrow transplant in order to save my life. That news broke them—I still can see them crying on my bed. *How in the world did we get here?!*

Unfortunately, there was more bad news to come. The cord blood that was saved from my sister's birth was only a haplo, or partial, match. All family members were tested, but no one was a complete match. The cord blood registry around the world was searched. My church even did a bone marrow registry drive, but the results were the same due to a unique gene in our family tree. Things got pretty bad, and they eventually decided to use the cord blood to do the transplant even though, at that time, using a haplo match was considered a risky procedure.

While in the hospital, I managed to make a friend, Vincent. He was sick like me, but we played with toys in the middle of the playroom and made a whole lot of noise. I remember those moments were the highlight of my stay at the hospital. One day we received the news that Vincent passed away. Many of the kids on my floor passed away. Those moments were scary because I wondered if it would be me one day.

It's amazing how some of my memories are so vivid! Whenever I would have a procedure, my dad promised me some money to go shopping when I got out of the hospital. There were only two things I wanted: money and Pokémon cards. I had so many albums of Pokémon cards. And everybody knew how much I loved money! Sometimes my dad would cry over having to leave me to go to work; that was tough. I watched my mommy pray for me through the good and bad days. I remember my family coming to spend time with me. My baby brother, Na'im, my Tias, Uncle Michael and Aunt Candi, and more. I really didn't look so good, especially when I lost all my hair. There were days when I was so weak, I couldn't even speak, and to sleep and eat was difficult. That never stopped my family, not even my tiny little sister. Everyone marveled at how I was able to withstand such pain. They would always tell me how brave and strong I was.

Who knew then that my baby sister, whom I adore and try to protect to this day, would make such a lasting impact by saving my life? After failed treatments, traditional and experimental, it came down to my sister's cord blood; the odds were not the highest, but God knew better. I went from death's door to surviving graph-versus-host disease (GVHD) and being strong enough to finish a charity marathon with my dad. My mom carried me to meet him at the finish line. I had to learn to do everything again!

Sure, I've said, "It's not fair!" I wanted to give up and stop trying many times over the years. I have cried out for a break, felt helpless, and even wanted out of my own skin. But remember, you can't judge a person before you walk in their shoes. I still struggle with side effects from the numerous treatments I endured during my journey. But Jesus struggled too! My family has never judged me and has always been there for me. When it gets tough, I remind myself that God sent an angel from heaven, my baby sister, Sydni, to shine a bright light of opportunity. The gift of my life resulted in our miracle story being published by the *Baltimore Sun*. The research that I participated in helped John Hopkins be recognized for completing the first successful cord blood transplant in Maryland.

My family has helped me recognize God's plan for my life. That is why I chose to share my story. I am now a twenty-five-year-old cancer survivor who wants to tell others this: Don't worry about yesterday, that's history! Tomorrow is always a mystery, which means you can still pull out a victory with God on your side! Recognize that it all starts with you. *The decision to RISE is yours!*

CONNECT WITH SHAWN "CASEY" COLLINS JR.

 @shawn.collins.10441

Arise & **SHINE**

Strategies to Live Empowered!

What have we learned journeying through these incredible stories of triumph? Well, you can safely say when it looks like every door is shut you can still arise and shine! Sometimes the hardest part is getting up but when you muster up the strength and lean on God - you can shout in victory "Then I Rise!" You must open your heart and mind to acknowledge there is a God for whom nothing is impossible. The key is inviting that power into your life.

What does it mean to Live Empowered? It is living with the knowledge that outside of you there is a never-ending power that [if you decide to tap into] will give you the strength to conquer any challenge placed in your path. That knowledge fuels and empowers you to live a life of activated faith. The stories in this book give us real world examples of courage, recovery, and restoration. Each experienced by people who were ready to fight for their lives. They are everyday heroes.

Here are some of the strategies that helped us to arise and shine and live empowered:

- Trust that God will help you rise. All you need to do is ask.
- Be ready to do the work required to achieve your goals—the process is unavoidable.
- Be courageous enough to ask yourself the right questions; taking on and conquering each of your limiting beliefs will surely empower your life.

- It is normal to doubt, but don't get stuck there. Push through using faith and trust as your tools to get to the other side of the difficulties life is sure to bring your way when you dare to live an empowered life.

- Remember always to leave room for God to show up and show out. He never disappoints.

- You have to deal with every stage of grief, or the pain will show up in other ways or areas of your life.

- Shame can be paralyzing, but faith has the power to break any chains that bind us. What seems insurmountable or unattainable can be the very table where God chooses to elevate you.

- Your story of shame, failure, and/or defeat can become a story of God's glory and a step-by-step example for others of how to overcome.

- Don't look to man for validation. You need only God's approval in life. That can be found through establishing a personal relationship with Him. Through prayer and worship, the gift of discernment will guide you and give your heart a sense of peace and the validation you seek.

- Never stop praying! Not just for yourself but for those around you, even those who persecute you.

- Don't lose sight of the fact that you can rise! We can easily succumb to who and what the world around us says we are and just sit in it; or you create your own truth when you decide to live an empowered life.

- Even when you are at your lowest, don't give it up. God will send you exactly who and what you need to persevere. Be open to accept His help and that of those He intentionally places in your path. Someone is waiting for your triumph story, but you must make healing your first priority. Only then can you be a blessing to someone else.

Remember you were born empowered, so don't allow anyone or anything to convince you not to Live Empowered! If you can see yourself in these pages, we hope you have discovered a blueprint to rise. If you have a story of triumph, we hope you choose to share it.

Continue your journey with us and become a member of the Life Empowered Movement by visiting www.ToniaBlackwood.com.

One Last Thing...

⭐⭐⭐⭐⭐

If this book has encouraged you to *arise and shine*, please take a moment to write a review. Please visit any **online bookseller** or **GoodReads.com**, search for this book and leave a review. It would also be an honor if you share this resource on any of your social media pages.

Your review does make a difference in helping others find this resource.

Help us spread the word! Please take a pic of you and your book and post it to social media using the hashtags #AriseAndShine and #ThenIRise.